D1689381

Bible Animal Stories
for Bedtime

Jane Landreth
Illustrated by David Miles

BARBOUR
PUBLISHING

© 2011 by Barbour Publishing, Inc.

All rights reserved. No part of this publication may be reproduced or transmitted for commercial purposes, except for brief quotations in printed reviews, without written permission of the publisher.

Churches and other noncommercial interests may reproduce portions of this book without the express written permission of Barbour Publishing, provided that the text does not exceed 500 words or 5 percent of the entire book, whichever is less and that the text is not material quoted from another publisher. When reproducing text from this book, include the following credit line: "From *Bible Animal Stories for Bedtime*, published by Barbour Publishing, Inc. Used by permission."

Scripture quotations marked NCV are taken from the New Century Version of the Bible, copyright © 2005 by Thomas Nelson, Inc. Used by permission.

Scripture quotations marked NIrV are taken from the HOLY BIBLE, NEW INTERNATIONAL READER'S VERSION™. Copyright © 1995, 1996, 1998 by International Bible Society. Used by permission of Zondervan. All rights reserved.

Scripture quotations marked NIV are taken from the HOLY BIBLE, NEW INTERNATIONAL VERSION®. NIV®. Copyright © 1973, 1978, 1984, 2010 by Biblica, Inc.™ Used by permission. All rights reserved worldwide.

Cover and interior illustrations by David Miles Illustration, www.davidmiles.com

Published by Barbour Publishing, Inc., P.O. Box 719, Uhrichsville, Ohio 44683, www.barbourbooks.com

Our mission is to publish and distribute inspirational products offering exceptional value and biblical encouragement to the masses.

ecpa Member of the Evangelical Christian Publishers Association

Printed in China.

"Ask the animals,
and they will teach you,
or the birds in the sky,
and they will tell you. . .
or let the fish of the sea
inform you."

Job 12:7–8 NIV

The Donkey Talks

The LORD made the donkey talk, and she said to Balaam,
"What have I done to make you hit me three times?"
NUMBERS 22:28 NCV

Donkeys love to roll over on the ground. One day a man named Balaam had a donkey. She didn't roll over but she did do some unusual things.

One day a king sent a message to Balaam. He would make Balaam rich if he would cause some bad things to happen to God's people.

Balaam saddled his donkey and traveled to see the bad king. God was angry with Balaam. So He sent an angel to block Balaam's way. The donkey left the road when she saw the angel. Balaam hit the donkey and got back on the road.

When the donkey saw the angel standing between two walls, she moved toward one wall. Balaam's foot was crushed. He hit the donkey again.

The third time the donkey saw the angel, she lay down. Balaam hit the donkey again.

God opened the donkey's mouth. "What have I done to make you hit me three times?" she said.

When Balaam started explaining why, God let him see the angel. The angel told Balaam that if the donkey had not turned away every time she saw the angel, the angel would have killed Balaam but saved the donkey!

Animals have their own way of communicating with each other and us. But if God needed an animal to actually talk, it would. God can do all things.

Dear God, You are truly the Master of me and all animals. Help me to be gentle with every living thing. Amen.

The Sheep, the Lion, and the Bear

But David said to Saul, "I've been taking care of my father's sheep. Sometimes a lion or a bear would come and carry off a sheep from the flock."

1 Samuel 17:34 NIrV

Lions can run up to fifty miles per hour! Bears are a little slower. They can run about thirty miles per hour. Both animals are a lot faster than we are! When a lion or a bear is hungry, it can attack another animal and make a fast getaway. So it was important for shepherds to keep a sharp eye on their sheep.

David watched his father's sheep. He would make sure the sheep had plenty of grass to eat and water to drink. He made sure no harm would come to them.

One day while David watched the

sheep, a bear charged the flock. It grabbed a sheep and carried it away. David raced after the bear and struck it with his shepherd's staff. The bear rushed toward David, but he was not afraid. He knew God would protect him. He grabbed the bear by its hair, struck it, and killed it.

Another day, a lion sneaked up on the sheep. It grabbed a sheep and took off. David raced after the lion and took the sheep out of its mouth. The hungry lion dashed after David. With God's help,

David grabbed the lion and killed it.

Bears and lions can be very fierce when hungry, but God protected David and his sheep, just like He protects us.

Dear God, thank You for helping us when we are in danger. With You by our side, we have the best protection ever. Amen.

The Wise Ants

Go watch the ants, you lazy person.
Watch what they do and be wise.
PROVERBS 6:6 NCV

A tiny ant is very strong! Depending on its species, an ant can lift and carry things that are three to twenty-five times its own weight! That is like you lifting three to twenty-five other kids your own size. That's strong! Ants live in colonies, much like a town. They depend on one another and help each other when they have a job to do. Working together, ants can find answers to hard problems.

In Bible times, wise men wrote many things that helped people make good choices. Solomon, a wise man, used the ant to show people how important it was to work together to get a job done well.

Solomon told lazy people to watch the ant. The ant goes out and looks for food. When it finds something, it lifts it and carries it back to its home. If something is too heavy for an ant to carry home, he calls other ants to come help. The ants store up food in their home so they will have something to eat when food is scarce.

We need to be wise like the ant—to work together to get things done. We also should always be prepared to help others—just like our friend, the ant.

Thank You, God, for the wise ant. Make me strong. Help me to work with other people to get things done well. Amen.

Shepherds Watch Their Sheep

That night, some shepherds were in the fields
nearby watching their sheep.
Luke 2:8 NCV

A sheep's coat is called a fleece. It keeps the sheep warm in the winter. In the summer, sheep shed their coat to keep cool. In Bible times, shepherds took their sheep into fields to eat fresh grass. Sometimes they would spend the night in the fields. One night while poor shepherds watched their sheep, something unusual happened.

Baa, baa. The sheep snuggled close together as the shepherds watched over them. Suddenly the sky became bright. An angel appeared and the shepherds were afraid.

"Don't be afraid," said the angel. "I bring you news that will bring you joy. In the city, a Savior has been born. You will find the baby wrapped in strips of cloth and lying in a manger."

Suddenly many angels appeared in the sky. They praised God and said, "Glory to God way up in heaven. Let there be peace among the people on earth who please God."

When the angels disappeared, one of the shepherds said, "Let's go to Bethlehem and see these things."

The shepherds found Mary, Joseph, and baby Jesus, just like the angels had told them. They returned to their sheep, praising God.

God used sheep-watching shepherds as the first messengers of Jesus' birth. God picks the lowliest of men for the greatest of deeds.

Dear God, thank You for baby Jesus. Please use me to tell others the good news. Amen.

A Net Full of Fish

When the fishermen did as Jesus told them,
they caught so many fish that the nets began to break.
Luke 5:6 NCV

God has created fish to travel in groups called schools. When fish swim in such large numbers, they are safer from animals that want to eat them. It would seem easier to catch a school of fish than just one fish. But that wasn't happening to some men in a boat on the Sea of Galilee.

When people began to crowd around Jesus, he got into a boat on the Sea of Galilee. He told Simon Peter to move the boat out into the water. Then Jesus began to teach the people.

Later that day, Jesus said to Simon, "Go out into the deep water. Let down the nets so you can catch some fish."

"Jesus, we fished all last night and caught nothing," answered Simon. "But we will do what You say."

Simon and the fishermen with him did what Jesus told them. They were surprised when they pulled up their nets full of fish. The nets were so full that they began to break.

"Come help us!" yelled Simon to the fishermen in a nearby boat.

The fishermen came and helped. They had so many fish they filled both boats! When we listen to Jesus, He blesses us beyond what we can imagine!

Dear God, thank You for all You have given me. Help me to share with others and to do what You tell me to do. Amen.

The Son and the Pigs

"The son wanted to fill his stomach with the food the pigs were eating."
Luke 15:16 NIrV

Pigs will eat almost anything—including worms, dead insects, tree bark, and garbage—yuck! Pigs are omnivores, which means they eat both plants and meat. One day a young man wanted to eat pig food!

A man had two sons. The younger son said to his father, "Give me part of your money. I don't want to wait until you die to get it."

The younger son took his money and traveled to a faraway land. He spent all his money having a good time. Soon he had no money left, not even for food to eat.

The son got a job feeding pigs. He was so hungry he wanted to eat the pigs' food.

Then he thought about his father. "Why am I here?" he said. "At home even the servants have plenty to eat. I will go home and tell my father I did wrong. I will ask for a job."

The father saw his son coming and ran to hug him.

"Father, I have done wrong," said the son.

The father called to his servants, "Quick! Bring my son the best robe, a ring for his finger, and shoes for his feet. Let's celebrate! My son has come home."

Like the son's father, God will always welcome us back, no matter what we've done!

Dear God, thank You for forgiving me. Tonight I will sleep well, knowing You will always welcome me with open arms. Amen.

The Lost Sheep

"He calls his friends and neighbors together and says,
'Rejoice with me; I have found my lost sheep.' "
LUKE 15:6 NIV

Sheep stay close together for protection. But if frightened, they will run in all directions. Sometimes a sheep will get lost. Jesus told a story about a lost sheep.

A shepherd had a hundred sheep. Every morning he would take his sheep to the hillsides. *Baa, baa,* went the sheep as they followed him. The sheep drank the cool water, ate the green grass, and rested in the shade. The shepherd loved his sheep and protected them.

When night came, the shepherd took his sheep to a pen called a sheepfold. The pen had no door so the shepherd slept across the doorway. "Nothing will hurt my sheep," he said.

Each night before he went to sleep, the shepherd counted his sheep. One night he began counting. "There's one, two, three, four, five. . ." He counted all the way to "Ninety-eight, ninety-nine. . ."

Suddenly the man stopped counting. One sheep was missing. "Lost sheep!" called the man. "Come to me!" The shepherd looked everywhere for his lost sheep.

Then he heard a quiet little sound. *Baa, baa.* There caught in a thorn bush was the lost sheep! The happy shepherd picked him up and carried him home on his shoulders.

Jesus is like that shepherd. If you ever stray, He will find you and bring you home!

Dear God, I am so glad that You are here to take care of me. I will never get lost if I stay close to You! Amen.

Dear God, thank You for making so many different kinds of creatures, including me! It's wonderful that we are not all the same. Amen.